The Titanic Disaster

PETER BENOIT

Children's Press®
An Imprint of Scholastic Inc.
New York Toronto London Auckland Sydney
Mexico City New Delhi Hong Kong
Danbury, Connecticut

Content Consultant
Paul F. Johnston, PhD
Maritime Historian
Washington, DC

Library of Congress Cataloging-in-Publication Data

Benoit, Peter, 1955–
  The Titanic disaster/Peter Benoit.
      p. cm.—(A true book)
  Includes bibliographical references and index.
ISBN-13: 978-0-531-20627-0 (lib. bdg.)   978-0-531-28996-9 (pbk.)
ISBN-10: 0-531-20627-0 (lib. bdg.)   0-531-28996-6 (pbk.)
  1. Titanic (Steamship)—Juvenile literature. 2. Shipwrecks—North Atlantic Ocean—History—20th century—Juvenile literature. I. Title. II. Series.
  G530.T6B56 2011
  910.9163'4—dc22   2010045932

All rights reserved. Published in 2011 by Children's Press, an imprint of Scholastic Inc.
Printed in USA. 08
SCHOLASTIC, CHILDREN'S PRESS, A TRUE BOOK and associated logos are trademarks and/or registered trademarks of Scholastic Inc.

  6 7 8 9 10 R 18 17 16 15 14 13 12

Find the Truth!

Everything you are about to read is true *except* for one of the sentences on this page.

Which one is **TRUE**?

T or F The *Titanic*'s radio was not operating the night the ship sank.

T or F In 1912, the *Titanic* was the largest steamer in the world.

Find the answers in this book.

TITANIC DISASTER GREAT LOSS OF LIFE
EVENING NEWS

Contents

THE BIG TRUTH!

Iceberg

RMS *Titanic*, Crown Jewel of the White Star Line

Some people played cards to pass the time on the *Titanic*.

**Survivor
Margaret
"Molly" Brown**

At the time the *Titanic* was built, many people thought it was a wonder of modern technology.

CHAPTER 1

Luxury Liner

On April 10, 1912, the RMS *Titanic* left the dock at Southampton, England, on its maiden, or first, voyage. The ship stretched almost 883 feet (269 meters) long and was 92 feet (28 m) wide. The people waving from the deck looked forward to pleasures no other ship could match. The *Titanic* offered everything from a gymnasium to cafés to libraries. A private radio even allowed passengers to send and receive messages—a **luxury** at the time.

← In 1912, the *Titanic* was the largest passenger ship in the world.

Rich and Poor

The millionaire John Jacob Astor IV and his wife were among the passengers on the *Titanic*. Other wealthy passengers wanted to be part of history by sailing on the world's greatest luxury liner. The poorer Goodwin family, meanwhile, headed to America to start a

John Jacob Astor IV and his wife

new life. The rich paid up to $4,350 per ticket, or more than $95,000 in today's dollars. The Goodwins, like hundreds of others, took a cheap third-class room deep inside the ship.

Power and Speed

The ship's 29 boilers and 159 furnaces propelled the ship at a then-quick 26 miles per hour (42 kilometers per hour). The size and speed of the ship created a powerful suction in the water behind it. When leaving Southampton, the *Titanic* pulled a smaller ocean liner away from the dock. The two ships barely avoided a collision.

Stops at Cherbourg, France, and Queenstown, Ireland, added more passengers. In all, more than 2,200 people set off across the Atlantic Ocean for New York.

RMS stands for Royal Mail Ship.

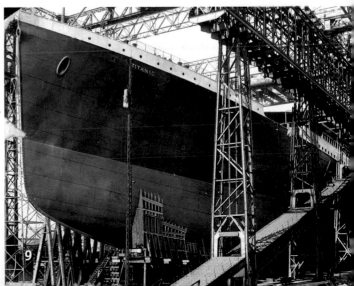

The *Titanic* was built in Belfast, Northern Ireland.

9

One of the ship's most
impressive features
was a grand staircase.

The Voyage

CHAPTER 2

The Voyage

The *Titanic* lived up to the promises. Ladies in fashionable clothes enjoyed afternoon tea. Gentlemen smoked pipes and talked business. In the evening, the Astors's supper might have begun with oysters and ended with ice cream or pudding. The Goodwins and other third-class passengers ate basic meals of roast beef, soup, and vegetables. Electric lights, another luxury, made it easy for everyone to admire the surroundings.

Polished oak and other fine details added to the luxury of the staircase.

11

Danger Ahead

On the night of April 14, the radio operators aboard the *Titanic* heard several messages warning of an ice field ahead. A ship usually slowed when it neared floating ice. But the *Titanic* sped ahead. The lookouts, watching without binoculars, stared into the dark. But the moonless night offered little light to see by. No one saw the iceberg dead ahead until it was too late.

Harold Bride (pictured in the *Titanic*'s radio room) was one of the ship's two radio operators.

Many smaller ships had only one radio operator.

It is difficult to tell the true size of an iceberg. Most of the ice is underwater.

Deadly Ice

Icebergs are islands of frozen freshwater that calve, or break off, from glaciers. In the North Atlantic, icebergs calve from Arctic glaciers. Currents and wind then carry the icebergs south. The largest icebergs tower 200 feet (60 m) above sea level. But most of an Arctic iceberg—on average, about 80 percent—is underwater. Ice can reach 1,000 feet (300 m) into the ocean depths.

CHAPTER 3

The Collision

As the *Titanic* neared the iceberg, lookout Frederick Fleet sounded the alarm. Fleet called the bridge and rang the ship's bell three times. The *Titanic* slowed and steered to one side. But the iceberg was too close. At 11:40 p.m., it scraped along the ship's **starboard** side. As the iceberg passed, the force from the moving ice caused the **rivets** holding the hull together to break loose. The hull's loosened metal plates bent inward. Water rushed into the ship.

Thomas Andrews, the *Titanic's* designer, went down with the ship. ➡

Planning for Disaster

The collision surprised the passengers. But they believed the *Titanic* could survive the impact. Thomas Andrews, the ship's designer, had designed the ship for safety. Vertical bulkhead, or walls, divided the hull into 16 areas, or compartments. The watertight doors of each compartment could be closed when a collision took place in order to keep water from flooding the ship. According to Andrews's plans, the *Titanic* would remain afloat even if four compartments filled with water. After the collision, however, water entered the first six compartments at the front of the ship.

After studying the damage, Andrews concluded the ship would sink in less than three hours.

No Panic Yet

Those still awake heard the iceberg grinding along the hull. Passengers on the deck watched the ice mountain pass and saw chunks of ice litter the deck. Many people in third class, meanwhile, had no idea what had happened. Rules kept them from leaving their area of the ship after 10 p.m., so they and their children were in bed. Even as the *Titanic* filled with water, some never got up.

Evidence suggests that the iceberg scraped several small slits in the hull of the *Titanic*, which led to the ship's sinking.

It took only minutes for water to flood the damaged compartments.

A special training drill had been set for April 14 to familiarize the ship's crew with the lifeboats. It was canceled.

Confusion

Confusion delayed the evacuation. Many people had trouble believing the ship could sink. The crew, meanwhile, lacked proper training. Though in charge of passenger safety, the crewmen had no idea what they were supposed to do in an emergency. Nearly an hour passed before the crew began to guide people to the only safe way off the ship: the lifeboats.

RMS *Titanic,* Crown Jewel of the White Star Line

The White Star Line designed the *Titanic* to impress because the company needed an eye-opening liner to compete with rivals. The builders, for example, added a fake fourth smokestack to make the ship look even more powerful. From the star-studded passenger list to the heated pool, the ship's maiden voyage was meant to grab attention.

18

Unsinkable

Denver millionaire Margaret Brown became famous for her bravery and for rescuing passengers. Newspapers nicknamed her the Unsinkable Molly Brown.

Stateroom

Wood paneling and fine furniture made staying in the first-class stateroom as pleasant as a visit to a fine hotel.

WHITE STAR LINE
ROYAL AND UNITED STATES Mail Steamer "BRITANNIC" (TRIPLE SCREW)
LAUNCHED AT BELFAST 26TH February 1914.

The sister ship of the *Titanic*, the HMHS *Britannic*, was just as long as and slightly wider than *Titanic*. *Britannic* sank in 1916 while being used as a World War I hospital ship.

Many who boarded
the lifeboats faced the
painful reality of saying
final good-byes to those
who were left behind.

CHAPTER 4

Women and Children First

The *Titanic* had only 20 lifeboats that together seated 1,178 passengers and crew—just half the people aboard. But as the *Titanic* took on water the passengers still waited to evacuate. No one knew what to do, including the crewmen. In third class, people waited for orders. Many were unclear on what had happened. As the crew finally prepared the first lifeboats, they began to choose passengers based on the rule "women and children first."

A large wooden lifeboat could carry 65 people.

Only 705 of 1,178 lifeboat spaces were used.

Lifeboats Away

The first lifeboat landed in the water an hour after the *Titanic* hit the iceberg. Only 28 people sat in a space that could fit 65 because both crew and passengers considered the lifeboats unsafe. As more women and children pressed forward, the crew continued to fill most lifeboats only partway. One of the small boats took only a dozen people when 40 would have fit.

The Final Lifeboats

By 1:15 a.m., seawater lapped at the name TITANIC painted on the ship's side. The *Titanic* leaned hard to its **port** side. The crew, despite their confusion, worked hard to launch all the lifeboats. The last boats tended to be more crowded as people realized what was happening. By 2:05 a.m., the last lifeboat left. More than 1,500 people, including most of the third-class passengers like the Goodwins, remained stranded on the ship.

Many who did not make it into lifeboats wore life jackets. They were able to float in the water, but died anyway of exposure to the icy waters.

Reactions Aboard

People aboard the *Titanic* reacted to the disaster in different ways. Many of the stories became famous in later years. John Jacob Astor, according to eyewitnesses, helped women into the lifeboats. Ida Straus refused a lifeboat

Captain Smith was set to retire soon after the *Titanic*'s maiden voyage.

seat, preferring to die with her husband, Isidor. Margaret Brown helped row away a lifeboat full of survivors. Captain Edward J. Smith, following naval **tradition**, went down with the ship.

The *Titanic's* Band

As passengers sought places in the lifeboats, eight musicians hired to entertain on the ship gathered on the deck. There, led by bandmaster Wallace Hartley, they played light and cheerful music. Survivors of the disaster claimed that the songs calmed frightened passengers. The band played past the departure of the last lifeboat and may have ended with the **hymn** "Nearer, My God, to Thee." None of the band members survived.

According to some survivors, Wallace Hartley continued to lead the musicians until the waves swept them overboard.

The Last Minutes

Icy water filled the rooms nearest the deck. Step by step it climbed the grand staircase. At 2:17 a.m., seawater rushed over the deck. Many of the people still on board dove into the ocean. The ship's **bow** dipped into the sea. A short time later, the **stern** rose from the water. The *Titanic* stood almost straight up. The lights dimmed and finally blinked out. Soon after, the *Titanic* broke into two pieces.

It took the *Titanic* roughly 10 minutes to reach bottom.

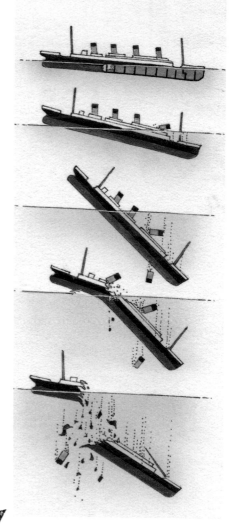

The *Titanic* broke in two because the ship could not handle the stress on its structure from having the stern in the air.

The bow of the ship sank first, followed soon after by the stern.

Hundreds of thrashing passengers screamed and called out from the water. But the lifeboats stayed away. Those in the boats worried the *Titanic*'s last plunge would suck them under, or that scared swimmers would tip over the lifeboats. In the end, only two of the lifeboats searched for survivors. The *Titanic*, meanwhile, sank with little suction. The cries from the water died away. The survivors faced a long night of cold and regret.

By some accounts, one reason the *Californian* didn't respond was because its radio operator had gone to bed.

CHAPTER 5

Mystery Ship

Before sinking, the *Titanic* put out calls for help over the radio. The crew also shot off flares to alert nearby ships. The nearest ship failed to answer. To this day, no one is sure of its identity. It was probably the steamer *Californian*. Later on, members of its crew admitted seeing distress flares from the *Titanic*. Other details suggest it was in the area. Why the captain may have ignored the signals is unknown.

← The *Californian* had stopped steaming for the night because of ice.

Aboard the *Carpathia*, many *Titanic* survivors were silent from the shock of the tragedy.

CHAPTER 6

The Rescue

Another passenger liner, the RMS *Carpathia*, answered the call from the *Titanic*. On being told of the distress signal, Arthur Henry Rostron, the *Carpathia*'s captain, ordered the ship to go to top speed. The *Carpathia* arrived around 4:10 a.m., less than two hours after the *Titanic* went down. By 8:30 a.m., the crew had pulled up the last survivors. The ship steamed immediately for New York.

One of the *Carpathia*'s dining rooms was used as a hospital area to treat the survivors.

A Shocking Event

News of what had happened traveled ahead of the *Carpathia*. A crowd waited when the ship pulled into New York on April 18. Already, the disaster had shocked the world. It seemed unthinkable that 1,517 people had lost their lives. Newspapers, meanwhile, rushed to print survivors' stories. When the real stories ran out, reporters made up a batch of new ones.

A torpedo sank the *Carpathia* during World War I.

John Jacob Astor IV, whose funeral is shown here, died in the sinking. Astor's was one of the few recovered bodies to be identified.

Sadness

While the survivors recovered from the disaster, the frozen bodies of the unluckier passengers were pulled from the Atlantic. Funerals helped friends and loved ones **mourn** the losses. The body of bandleader Wallace Hartley was returned with honor to his hometown. On May 18, more than 30,000 mourners attended Hartley's funeral. The music for "Nearer, My God, to Thee" was carved onto his tombstone.

The Investigation

People throughout the United States and Great Britain demanded answers. What had gone wrong? A court looking into the disaster found some disturbing answers. Soon the public learned that the radio operators had ignored warnings of ice ahead, that no one had given binoculars to the lookouts, and that the captain had sped into the ice field. The crew's lack of training also came to light, as did the fact that the *Californian* had apparently ignored the *Titanic*'s distress signals.

Timeline of the *Titanic* Story

1909
Builders begin the *Titanic*.

1911
The *Titanic* is completed.

Accident and Error

The investigation turned up other problems with the *Titanic* herself. It turned out the rivets used to fasten the hull together were weaker than the builders believed. In addition, some criticized the decision to turn away from the iceberg. The critics thought Captain Smith should have rammed the ice. A head-on collision, they said, would have flooded only two compartments—not enough to sink the ship.

1912
The *Titanic* sinks on its maiden voyage.

1985
Robert D. Ballard helps lead the team that locates the shipwreck.

Helping and Remembering

The investigators concluded a mix of bad luck and human error led to the disaster. Charities sprang up to help those who had lost loved ones on the *Titanic*. In both the United States and Great Britain, people organized memorials to remember the passengers and crew. One of the most famous was dedicated to the musicians. Isidor Straus's sons built a hall at Harvard University in his honor.

The Titanic Engineers Memorial is located in Southampton, England. It honors the many engineer officers who went down with the ship.

Retelling the Story

The first *Titanic* film, *In Night and Ice*, came out in 1912. *A Night to Remember* was a hit in 1958. Margaret Brown's life became the Broadway show *The Unsinkable Molly Brown* in 1960. In 1997, the movie *Titanic* broke box office records. By far the strangest *Titanic* story was Morgan Robertson's *Futility*. The novel told how an iceberg sank a liner named *Titan*. Robertson, however, wrote his tale in 1898 — 14 years before *Titanic*'s voyage.

At the time of its release, *Titanic* was the most expensive film ever made.

Titanic (1997) movie poster

Since the discovery of the ship's remains, many trips have been made to the *Titanic* wreck.

CHAPTER 7

Finding the *Titanic*

For decades, the exact location of the *Titanic* wreck remained a mystery. Experts had to search a wide area. Sending cameras to the ocean bottom was a challenge. In 1985, Robert D. Ballard led a team that pulled a **sonar** and video camera system through the deep water. There, more than 12,400 feet (3,780 m) down, the Ballard team spotted **debris** from the *Titanic*.

A century from now, the *Titanic* may be nothing more than a pile of rust.

Exploring the Wreck

After the 1985 discovery, several expeditions had a look at the wreckage on the ocean floor. In 1987, a company called RMS Titanic, Inc., made the first of its seven explorations. Seven years later, a U.S. court gave the company rights to **salvage** items from and pieces of the *Titanic*. RMS Titanic, Inc., has since brought up **artifacts** such as dishes, playing cards, and jewelry.

Titanic playing cards featured the White Star Line logo.

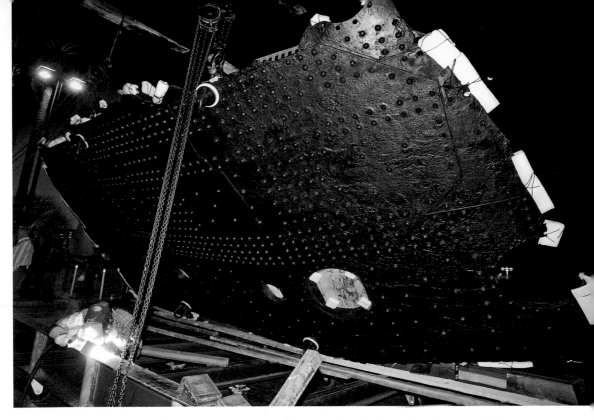

Some of the portholes (small round windows) of the Big Piece still have the original glass.

The largest item salvaged thus far is a 17-ton section of the hull nicknamed the Big Piece. In 1996, an expedition attached floating oil-filled bags to the Big Piece and pulled it from the seafloor. But bad weather caused the chains and cables holding the Big Piece to break. It sank. Two years later, a second expedition pulled it up again, this time for good.

Not Yet at Rest

Private submarines now take tourists to see the wreck. In fact, it's possible the *Titanic* story is too popular. Ballard and other experts blame the large number of visitors for damaging the ship, littering the area, and taking artifacts. A hundred years after the *Titanic* sank, people are still curious about one of history's most famous sea disasters. ★

Tourist submarines can damage the *Titanic* when they land or bump into the ship.

A craft, containing two tourists and a pilot, prepares to visit the *Titanic* wreck.

True Statistics

Size of the RMS *Titanic*: Almost 883 ft. (269 m) long and 92 ft. (28 m) wide

Engine power source: 29 boilers fueled by 159 coal furnaces

Top speed: 26 mph (42 kph)

Number of people aboard: More than 2,200

Time of collision with an iceberg: 11:40 p.m., April 14, 1912

Number of lifeboats on board: 20

Number of people killed: 1,517

Did you find the truth?

F The *Titanic*'s radio was not operating the night the ship sank.

T In 1912, the *Titanic* was the largest steamer in the world.

The World.

REAT TITANIC SINKS; MORE THAN 1,500 LOST;
866 WOMEN AND CHILDREN KNOWN TO BE SAVED;
SCORES OF NOTABLES NOT ACCOUNTED FOR

LIST OF THE KNOWN SAVED

Front page of a newspaper headlining the *Titanic* disaster

Resources

Books

Adams, Simon. *Titanic*. New York: DK Publishing, 2009.

Brown, Don. *All Stations! Distress!: April 15, 1912, the Day the Titanic Sank*. New York: Flash Point/Roaring Brook Press, 2008.

Caper, William. *Nightmare on the Titanic*. New York: Bearport Publishing Company, 2007.

Crosbie, Duncan. *Titanic: The Ship of Dreams*. New York: Orchard Books, 2007.

Fahey, Kathleen. *Titanic*. Milwaukee: Gareth Stevens Publishing, 2005.

Green, Jen. *Atlantic Ocean*. Milwaukee: World Almanac Library, 2006.

Hall, Kirsten. *Deep Sea Adventures: A Chapter Book*. New York: Children's Press, 2003.

Jenkins, Martin. *Titanic*. Cambridge, MA: Candlewick Press, 2008.

Molony, Senan. *Titanic: A Primary Source History*. Milwaukee: Gareth Stevens Publishing, 2006.

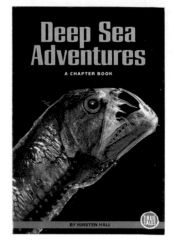

Organizations and Web Sites

Discovery Channel: Last Mysteries of the Titanic
http://dsc.discovery.com/convergence/titanic/titanic.html
Do fun activities and learn more about one of history's most famous ships.

History.com: Titanic Interactive
www.history.com/interactives/titanic-interactive
Learn more about the construction of the *Titanic* and take a virtual tour of the ship.

National Geographic Explorer: Return to Titanic
http://magma.nationalgeographic.com/ngexplorer/0411/articles/mainarticle.html
Find lots of facts and information about the *Titanic* at this Web site.

Places to Visit

Titanic Memorial
Waterfront Park near
4th Street
Washington, DC 20024
www.glts.org/memorials/dc/womens.html
This is a dramatic monument to those who died in the disaster.

Titanic Museum
3235 76 Country Blvd &
Hwy 165
Branson, MO 65616-3551
(417) 334-9500
www.titanicbranson.com
Visitors walk inside a copy of the original *Titanic*.

Important Words

artifacts (ART-uh-fakts)—objects from a past time

bow (BOU)—the front of a ship

debris (duh-BREE)—the remains of something that has been destroyed

hymn (HIM)—a piece of religious music

luxury (LUHK-shuh-ree)—something that adds to comfort or pleasure

mourn (MORN)—to be sad over the death of someone or something

port (PORT)—the left side of a ship when one is facing forward; also a harbor town and a window aboard a ship or boat

rivets (RIV-its)—bolts of metal used to fasten two pieces of metal together

salvage (SAL-vij)—to recover from a wreck or ruin

sonar (SOH-nar)—a device that finds objects using sound waves

starboard (STAR-burd)—the right side of a ship when one is facing forward

stern (STERN)—the rear of a ship

tradition (trah-DISH-uhn)—a pattern of thought or action

Index

Page numbers in **bold** indicate illustrations

About the Author

Peter Benoit is educated as a mathematician but has many other interests. He has taught and tutored high school and college students for many years, mostly in math and science. He also runs summer workshops for writers and students of literature. Mr. Benoit has also written more than 2,000 poems. His life has been one committed to learning. He lives in Greenwich, New York.